MAKING 10

By CHARLES GHIGNA

Illustrations by MISA SABURI

Music by ERIK KOSKINEN

CANTATA LEARNING

WWW.CANTATALEARNING.COM

CANTATA LEARNING

Published by Cantata Learning
1710 Roe Crest Drive
North Mankato, MN 56003
www.cantatalearning.com

Library of Congress Cataloging-in-Publication Data
Names: Ghigna, Charles, author. | Saburi, Misa, illustrator. | Koskinen,
  Erik, composer.
Title: Making 10 / by Charles Ghigna ; illustrations by Misa Saburi ; music
  by Erik Koskinen.
Other titles: Making ten
Description: North Mankato, MN : Cantata Learning, [2017] | Series: Winter
  math | Audience: Ages 3-8. | Audience: K to grade 3. | Description based
  on print version record and CIP data provided by publisher; resource not
  viewed.
Identifiers: LCCN 2017007520 (print) | LCCN 2017013997 (ebook) | ISBN
  9781684100385 | ISBN 9781684100378 (hardcover : alk. paper)
Subjects: LCSH: Counting--Juvenile literature. | Winter--Juvenile
literature.
Classification: LCC QA113 (ebook) | LCC QA113 .G47455 2017 (print) | DDC
  513.2/11--dc23
LC record available at https://lccn.loc.gov/2017007520

Book design, Tim Palin Creative
Editorial direction, Flat Sole Studio
Executive musical production and direction, Elizabeth Draper
Music arranged and produced by Erik Koskinen

Printed in the United States of America in North Mankato, Minnesota.
072017   0367CGF17

ACCESS THE MUSIC!

SCAN
CODE
WITH
MOBILE
APP

CANTATALEARNING.COM

TIPS TO SUPPORT LITERACY AT HOME

WHY READING AND SINGING WITH YOUR CHILD IS SO IMPORTANT

Daily reading with your child leads to increased academic achievement. Music and songs, specifically rhyming songs, are a fun and easy way to build early literacy and language development. Music skills correlate significantly with both phonological awareness and reading development. Singing helps build vocabulary and speech development. And reading and appreciating music together is a wonderful way to strengthen your relationship.

READ AND SING EVERY DAY!

TIPS FOR USING CANTATA LEARNING BOOKS AND SONGS DURING YOUR DAILY STORY TIME

1. As you sing and read, point out the different words on the page that rhyme. Suggest other words that rhyme.

2. Memorize simple rhymes such as Itsy Bitsy Spider and sing them together. This encourages comprehension skills and early literacy skills.

3. Use the questions in the back of each book to guide your singing and storytelling.

4. Read the included sheet music with your child while you listen to the song. How do the music notes correlate to the words of the song?

5. Sing along on the go and at home. Access music by scanning the QR code on each Cantata book. You can also stream or download the music for free to your computer, smartphone, or mobile device.

Devoting time to daily reading shows that you are available for your child. Together, you are building language, literacy, and listening skills.

Have fun reading and singing!

The winter season is a time to see and do all sorts of fun things. You can make snow angels and drink cups of hot cocoa. You can **decorate** trees and watch snowflakes fall. Learn to count from 1 to 10 by counting the things you see.

Turn the page to **practice** counting to 10. Remember to sing along!

We count numbers, 1 to 10.

We like counting with a friend!

1 little snowball
down by the lake.

2 little snowballs—

what can we make?

3 little snowballs—
1, 2, and 3!

We made a snowman.
Come here and see.

4 laughing children
play in the snow.

See the snow angels
all in a row!

5 flying geese **soar** way up high.

6 speeding skaters zipping by.

7 **steaming** cups
of hot cocoa.

8 melting globs
    of marshmallows.

9 snowy trees
are all **aglow**.

18

10 pretty snowflakes
by the window!

19

We count numbers, 1 to 10.
We like counting with a friend!
1, 2, 3, 4, 5, 6, 7, 8, 9, 10!

Come on friends,
let's count them again.
1, 2, 3, 4, 5, 6, 7, 8, 9, 10!

SONG LYRICS
Making 10

We count numbers, 1 to 10.
We like counting with a friend!

1 little snowball
    down by the lake.
2 little snowballs—
    what can we make?

3 little snowballs—
    1, 2, and 3!
We made a snowman.
    Come here and see.

4 laughing children
    play in the snow.
See the snow angels
    all in a row!

5 flying geese
    soar way up high.
6 speeding skaters
    zipping by.

7 steaming cups
    of hot cocoa.
8 melting globs
    of marshmallows.

9 snowy trees
    are all aglow.
10 pretty snowflakes
    by the window!

We count numbers, 1 to 10.
We like counting with a friend!
1, 2, 3, 4, 5, 6, 7, 8, 9, 10!

Come on friends,
let's count them again.
1, 2, 3, 4, 5, 6, 7, 8, 9, 10!

Making 10

Americana
Erik Koskinen

Verse

1. We count num-bers, one to ten. We like count-ing with a friend!

Verse 2

1 lit-tle snow-ball down by the lake.
2 lit-tle snow-balls—what can we make?

Chorus

Three lit-tle snow-balls—one, two, and three! We made a snow-man. Come here and see.

Verse 3

4 laughing children play in the snow.
See the snow angels all in a row!

Chorus

7 steaming cups of hot cocoa.
8 melting globs of marshmallows.

Chorus

We count numbers, 1 to 10.
We like counting with a friend!

Verse 4

5 flying geese soar way up high.
6 speeding skaters zipping by.

Verse 5

9 snowy trees are all aglow.
10 pretty snowflakes by the window!

Outro

One, two, three, four, five, six, sev-en, eight, nine, ten! Come on friends, let's count them a-gain.

One, two, three, four, five, six, sev-en, eight, nine, ten!

23

GLOSSARY

aglow—giving off a steady, low light

decorate—to make more attractive and beautiful

practice—to do something over and over again to get it right

soar—to fly up high

steaming—hot and giving off steam or water vapor

GUIDED READING ACTIVITIES

1. What is winter like where you live? Is it warm or cold? Is it snowy or rainy? What type of clothes do you wear to play outside?

2. Now that you have counted from 1 to 10, try counting backwards. Start with the number 10 and then count back to 1.

3. Draw a winter scene. See if you can include 1 of something, 2 of something, 3 of something, all the way up to 10 of something.

TO LEARN MORE

Rustad, Martha E. H. *100 Snowflakes: A Winter Counting Book*. Mankato, MN: Amicus, 2017.

McKellar, Danica. *Goodnight, Numbers!* New York: Crown Books, 2017.

Higgins, Nadia. *Count It!* Minneapolis: Pogo, 2017.

Moon, Walt K. *Winter Is Fun!* Minneapolis: Lerner Publications, 2017.